THE ORGANIC BUG BOOK

Written and Illustrated
by CHRIS KORROW

Lindisfarne Books
2013

Lindisfarne Books
An imprint of SteinerBooks
610 Main Street, Great Barrington, MA 01230
www.steinerbooks.org

Library of Congress Cataloging-in-Publication Data

Korrow, Chris.
The organic bug book / written and illustrated [by] Chris Korrow. – 1st ed.
p. cm.
ISBN 978-1-58420-145-8 (pbk.) – ISBN 978-1-58420-146-5 (e-book)
1. Beneficial insects – Juvenile literature. 2. Insects – Juvenile literature.
3. Organic gardening – Juvenile literature. I. Title.
SF517.K67 2013
628.9'657 – dc23
2013007268

Printed in the United States of America

This book is dedicated to all creatures, great *and* small,
with whom we share this planet—might as
well include everybody!

There are about 1,400,000 different documented species of animals on Earth. Almost 1,000,000 of those are insects and 100,000 are arachnids (spiders, scorpions, ticks, mites).

Once upon a time there was a farmer named Chris, who was fascinated by the world of insects.

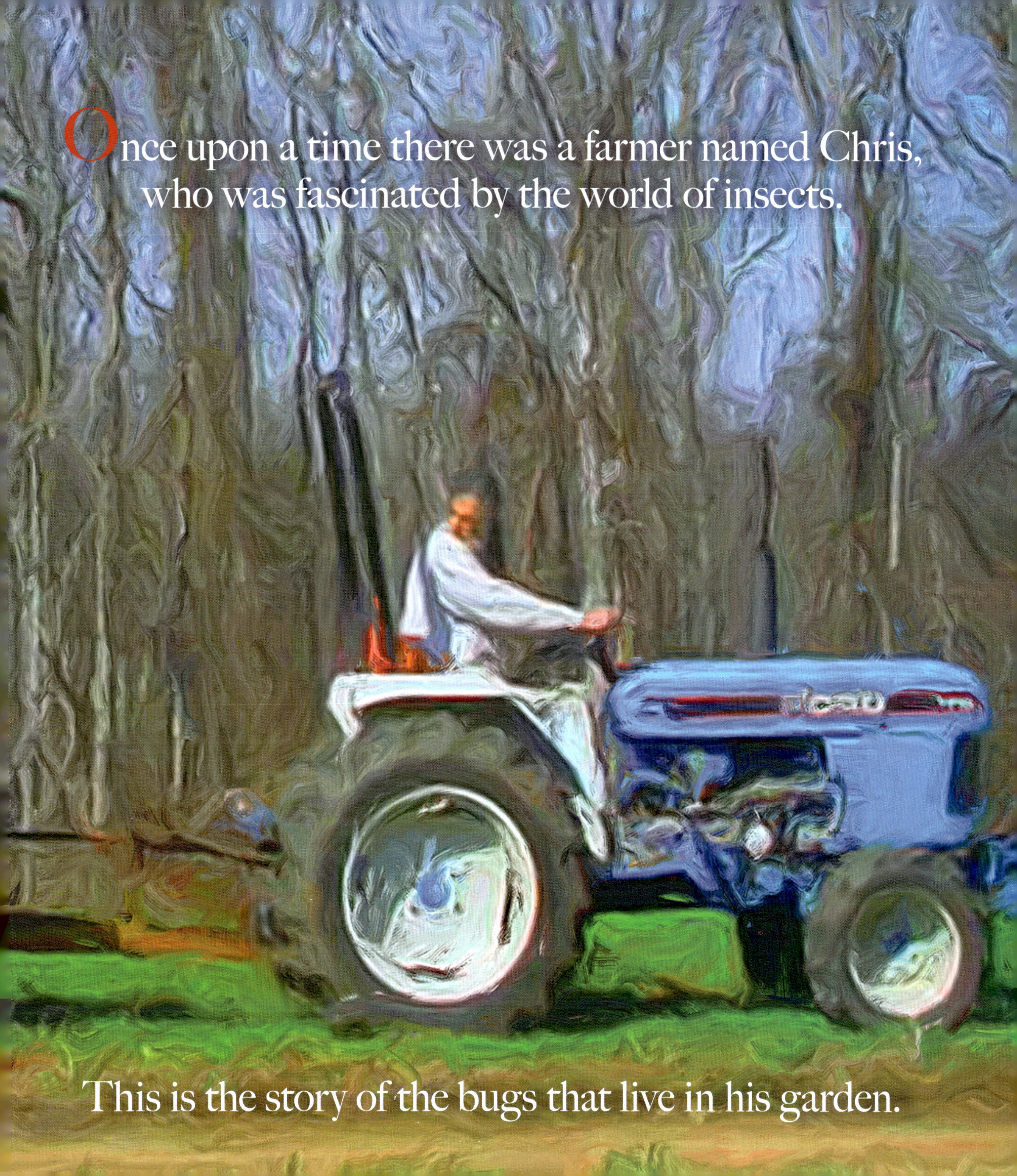

This is the story of the bugs that live in his garden.

FLIES are one of the most misunderstood of garden insects. We look at them as dirty, nasty creatures, but almost all of the flies in our gardens are beneficial, because they are predators. Their young are called larvae and they eat garden pests.

HOVERFLIES can remain perfectly still while in mid-flight. They are probably the most common kind of predatory fly in the garden. Their larvae feed on aphids and other plant-sucking insects.

This PREDATORY TACHINID FLY could easily be mistaken for a housefly.

One of the most interesting flies is the ROBBER FLY, which feeds on a large variety of insects. I have seen them in flight with grasshoppers that are much bigger than they are.

Bugs. The word alone evokes disgust in many people.

The Farmer

Most people live a relatively bug-free existence, but they are a major part of mine.

Praying Mantis

LIGHTNING BUGS

Their blinking light shows fill both children and adults with wonder. Lightning bugs primarily eat pollen, but their larvae spend their lives in the soil feeding on pests.

PRAYING MANTIS

There are only about 20 different species of mantises in North America, and they are at the top of the insect food chain, with few enemies. This can make them quite tame and fairly unafraid of an open hand. But don't grab one, because they can pinch.

They are my friends,

APHIDS are incredibly prolific. They can increase in number from just a few to thousands in a very short period of time. They are found throughout the garden during most of the year, sucking juices from plants. In a healthy garden, there is an abundance of predators to keep them in check.

GRASSHOPPERS are a much more diverse group than they are given credit for. They come in many colors and sizes and can jump twenty times their length.

FLEA BEETLES are a real nuisance to crops. Unprotected seedlings can quickly be devoured by this tiny pest.

This STINK BUG and its foul smelling relatives are common pests that suck the juice of plants.

my enemies,

A welcome visitor to the skies over my garden, the DRAGONFLY eats on the wing, snatching up mosquitoes and other small flying insects.

JUMPING SPIDERS are my favorite arachnid. They seem to have the most personality of the bunch. They don't make webs, and they travel widely in search of food. They have the best eyesight of all the spiders.

and my companions.

The PILL BUG is actually related to crabs and lobsters, and breathes with gills!

Look at how the droplets of water have collected on the wings of this APHID.

This red and black WEEVIL and this bright yellow ASSASSIN BUG are examples of how beautiful and colorful insects can be.

They inspire me.

Leather Wing

Horned Beetle

Asparagus Beetle

Lady Bug Larvae

BEETLES

Here are a few examples of one of the largest and most diverse orders of the insect class. There are over 300,000 different beetle species in the world, making up one third of all insects.

Mexican Bean Beetle

Locust Borer

They overwhelm me with their abundance and diversity.

Harlequin Bug

The SQUASH BUG injects fluids into the plant before feeding. These digestive juices are devastating to squash plants.

The SPOTTED CUCUMBER BEETLE doesn't kill the cucumber and melon plants by feeding on them, but by spreading disease among them.

CABBAGE LOPER CATERPILLARS can be real pests when their larva infest cabbage and broccoli plants.

They have caused me a tremendous amount of work, frustration ,

Red Wasp

SWEAT BEES

Though these tiny bees are helpful in pollination, they can be a real pain. They are attracted to the salt in human sweat. I can get stung twenty or thirty times while digging potatoes!

RED WASP OR PAPER WASP

Where did we get the idea for paper? Maybe it was from wasps. They have been making paper nests for thousands of years.

and pain.

In spring, babies will hatch out of a PRAYING MANTIS EGG CASE attached to a tall weed. Before mowing a field, I have often collected the styrofoam-like egg cases and relocated them to safety near the edge of the garden.

LADY BUGS are a gardener's friend. Why? One reason is because they eat aphids, which are among the most destructive of garden pests. There are farm supply companies that sell lady bugs, and they will send you a bag of lady bugs in the mail!

POTATO BEETLES lay their eggs on the underside of potato leaves. When the eggs hatch, their larvae begin to eat the potato leaves.

I have killed them, saved them, and even bought them.

Giant Swallowtail

Great Spangled Fritillary

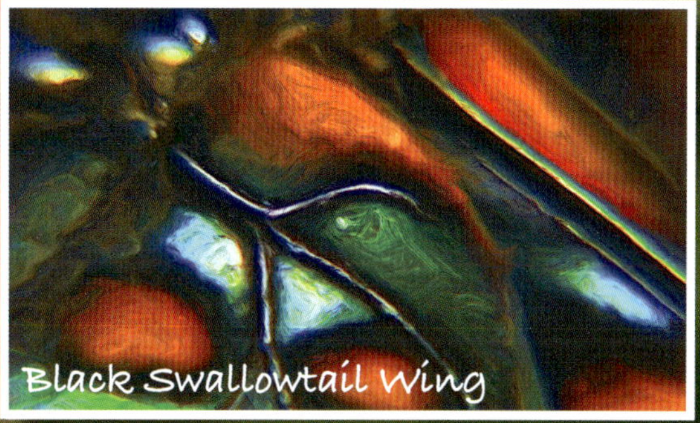

Black Swallowtail Wing

American Painted Lady

Painted Lady

When disturbed, the EASTERN BLACK or PARSLEY SWALLOWTAIL CATERPILLAR produces a strong smell from its two orange horns. More of an oddity than a threat, it munches on carrots, parsley, and other related species.

They bring wonder and joy on the wings of butterflies.

SPIDERWEBS catch more than just insects. Look closely and you may see them catch dewdrops, or even sunshine.

SPIDERS

One of the most efficient predators of garden pests, they have developed gossamer silk stronger than steel, paralyzing venom to immobilize their prey, and an incredible diversity of shapes, sizes, and colors.

Yet the occasional scorpion can still give me a touch of the willies!

They are a part of my life like the flowers in spring,

and they have made me a better human being

BEES

Almost all fruit and grain crops require pollination, and the honey bee is responsible for most of that pollination. There are also more than 3,500 species of solitary bees in North America that are busy-as-a-bee pollinating plants. No pollination, no seed—no seed, no plants. So, thank the bees for keeping the world green.

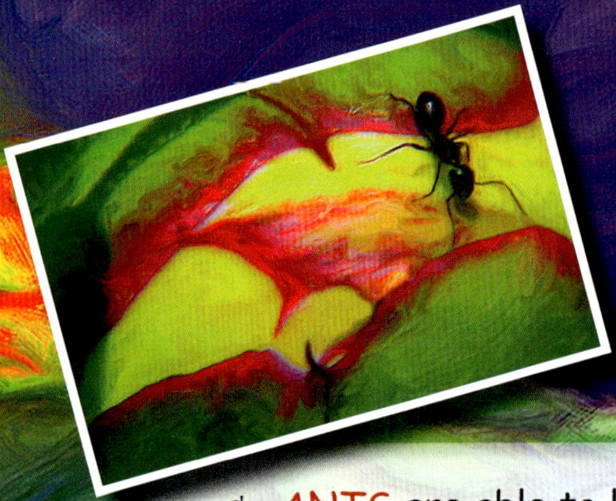

ANTS are able to lift and move many times their own weight. Ants work as a group to build their nests in the ground, moving literally tons of dirt. Transporting it grain by grain, these tiny bulldozers help to loosen and aerate the soil.

by showing me that they are not insignificant,

just small and numerous.

How many bugs can you name?

20
14
19
17
15
18
21
16
24
23
25
22
28
29
27
31
26
32
30
36
34
35
33
37
38

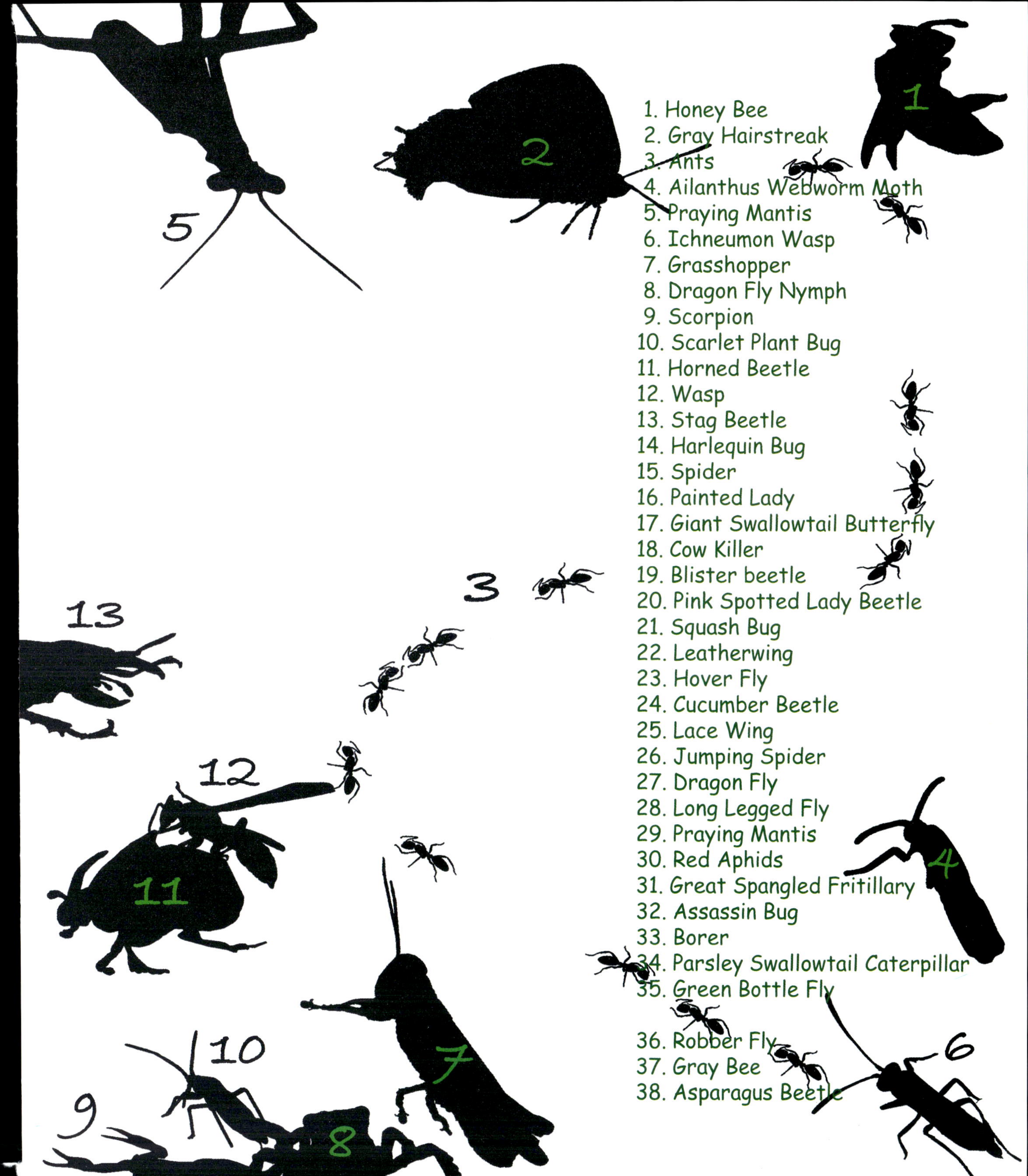

1. Honey Bee
2. Gray Hairstreak
3. Ants
4. Ailanthus Webworm Moth
5. Praying Mantis
6. Ichneumon Wasp
7. Grasshopper
8. Dragon Fly Nymph
9. Scorpion
10. Scarlet Plant Bug
11. Horned Beetle
12. Wasp
13. Stag Beetle
14. Harlequin Bug
15. Spider
16. Painted Lady
17. Giant Swallowtail Butterfly
18. Cow Killer
19. Blister beetle
20. Pink Spotted Lady Beetle
21. Squash Bug
22. Leatherwing
23. Hover Fly
24. Cucumber Beetle
25. Lace Wing
26. Jumping Spider
27. Dragon Fly
28. Long Legged Fly
29. Praying Mantis
30. Red Aphids
31. Great Spangled Fritillary
32. Assassin Bug
33. Borer
34. Parsley Swallowtail Caterpillar
35. Green Bottle Fly
36. Robber Fly
37. Gray Bee
38. Asparagus Beetle

RESOURCES FOR PARENTS

Tips for Organic Pest Control

Observe:
Begin by considering that there is a reason for every creature and every process in the garden. More than just growing plants, the gardener is managing an entire ecosystem, so the gardener must have an awareness of what is happening in the garden. How to do this? It's simple—spend time in the garden, watching and observing. If you notice insect damage, check under the leaves of the plants, poke around in the soil at the base of the plants. You'll be surprised at how much you can learn about insect pests.

Compost:
A garden system works from the bottom up, starting with healthy soil. Designed by nature, compost can be considered food for the soil. In the forest, leaves fall to the ground and are transformed into humus that is rich with nutrients and micro-organisms. This organic material provides a balanced diet for the trees and other flora. Compost is a our way of mimicking the sustainable fertility found in nature. Garden compost can be created from kitchen waste (minus meat and dairy), combined with grass clippings and other garden waste. Even better, visit a local farmer and carry home some hay, straw, and cow manure to add to your pile! Think of compost as a way to build your garden's immune system, which helps plants withstand insect damage.

Hand Pick:
A simple way to keep some insect pests in check is to pick them off by hand and squish them (yes squish), or shake them into a bucket with a couple of inches of water at the bottom. This works especially well with potato beetles.

Grow Varieties Suitable to Your Region:
One of the most important tasks of good farmers is to trial different plant varieties, to find the ones that are best suited to their area and their specific soil. So don't just settle for typical seedlings sold at the local garden center. Find out what organic farmers are growing in your area. To get the best plants for your area, you may have to start some of your own plants from seed. Farmers also love to pass along their knowledge to interested listeners.

Don't Spray:
There is a common misconception about organics—that it is just about gardening without chemicals. It's really about our connection with the world and our gardens. As for spraying insecticide—with the exception of a few organic, botanically-based products—if it kills all the bugs, it is also harmful to other living beings, from microscopic soil bacteria to children. There are many options for dealing organically with persistent insect pests, from planting enough for everyone to the use of organic sprays.

Appreciate:
If you see a bug (or a flower, or anything in nature for that matter) let go of your hurry. Stop and watch (be with it) for a while, even if it's not "doing" anything. Nature provides a wonderful environment in which we can learn and discover. Time in the garden melts away stress, and renews our body and our thoughts. It has a profound effect on us that is an antidote to the hours spent in front of television and computer.

- *Garden Insects* (DVD by Chris Korrow) www.gardeninsectvideo.com
- FEDCO Seeds, near Waterville, Maine. A seed cooperative committed to open-pollinated varieties and non-GMO seeds. www.fedcoseeds.com
- Local Harvest. An amazing data base of local farms throughout the US who sell food. www.localharvest.org
- *Gardening for Life: The Biodynamic Way* by Maria Thun, Available from SteinerBooks. wwwsteinerbooks.org. Maria Thun (1922–2012) was a German farmer who gardened biodynamically for over 50 years. This book is filled with practical, basic information from a true expert.